Six Stories
& an essay

By Andrea Levy and available from Headline

EVERY LIGHT IN THE HOUSE BURNIN'

NEVER FAR FROM NOWHERE

FRUIT OF THE LEMON

SMALL ISLAND

THE LONG SONG

SIX STORIES AND AN ESSAY

Six Stories & an essay

ANDREA LEVY

TINDER
PRESS

First published in 2014 by TINDER PRESS

An imprint of HEADLINE PUBLISHING GROUP

1

Cataloguing in Publication Data is available from the British Library

Hardback ISBN 978 1 4722 2266 4

Typeset in Bembo by Avon DataSet Ltd, Bidford on Avon, Warwickshire
Printed and bound in Great Britain by Clays Ltd St Ives plc

Papers used by Headline are from well-managed forests
and other responsible sources.

HEADLINE PUBLISHING GROUP
An Hachette UK Company
338 Euston Road
London NW1 3BH

www.tinderpress.co.uk
www.headline.co.uk
www.hachette.co.uk

For my family.

For my friends.

I would like to thank Bill Mayblin for all his help and careful comments during the writing of the essay *Back to My Own Country* and *Uriah's War*.

Two books were invaluable in the researching of *Uriah's War*:

Smith, Richard – *Jamaican Volunteers in the First World War. Race, masculinity and the development of national consciousness.*

Cundall, F – *Jamaica's Part in the Great War 1914– 1918 (published, Jamaica 1925)*

And lastly, I would like to acknowledge the great debt that I owe to my lovely mum, Amy Levy.

CONTENTS

LIST OF
ILLUSTRATIONS

Back to My Own Country

an essay

I REMEMBER A JOURNEY I took on a London bus when I was a young girl. It was in the early nineteen sixties. The bus was full of people and one of them was a black man. That was not a common sight in those days. I could tell from his accent that, like my parents, he was from somewhere in the Caribbean. He was talkative, smiling politely at people and trying to engage them in chat. But all the other people on the bus were white and they were looking at him askance. Nobody would be drawn into conversation; they clearly wanted nothing to do with him. But he carried on trying anyway.

I was embarrassed by him, but also overcome with pity for his hopeless attempt to be friendly on a London bus. I was sure that he was a nice man and that if those people on the bus could just get to know him then they would like him. My family also came from the Caribbean. I identified with him. He somehow became my mum and dad, my sisters, my brother, me. But to the other people on the bus he was more than a stranger, he was an alien. I felt a longing to make some introductions. I could sense the misunderstandings that were taking place, but I didn't know why, or what I could do. The man was different. He looked different and he sounded different. But how come people in England did not know him? Why was he, and why were all black people from Britain's old empire, so completely alien to them? This encounter is something I will never forget.

The same thing would not happen today in quite that way. Everyone is used to a mix of cultures and London buses are full of Londoners from all over the world. But still there are silences and gaps in our knowledge and understanding. What are the links that made Britain a natural destination for that Caribbean man on the bus, fifty years ago? How and why did Britain forge those links in the first place? These are questions that have come to fascinate me, because they reveal what amounts to a lost history for many of us. It was certainly lost to me for much of my early life, and it was a loss that caused me some problems.

At the time of my bus ride I lived on a council estate in north London. I went to a local school. Spoke like a good cockney. I played outside with all the white kids who lived around my way – rounders, skipping and hide and seek. I ate a lot of sweets. Watched a lot of television: *Coronation Street*, *Emergency Ward 10*. Loved the Arsenal. Hated Tottenham Hotspur. I lived the life of an ordinary London working-class girl.

But my parents had come to this country from Jamaica. And in the area of London where we lived, that made my family very odd. We were immigrants. Outsiders. My dad had been a passenger on the *Empire Windrush* ship when it famously sailed into Tilbury in June 1948 and, according to many, changed the face of Britain for ever. My mum came to England on a Jamaica Banana Producer's boat. It sailed into West India dock on Guy Fawkes Night in the same year, under a shower of fireworks that my mum believed were to welcome her.

My dad was an accounting clerk in Jamaica for, among other companies, Tate & Lyle. My mum was a teacher. They were middle class. They grew up in large houses. They even had servants. They came to Britain on British Empire passports in order to find more opportunities for work and advancement. But once here they struggled to find good housing. They had to live in one room for many years. They had a period of being homeless and then living in half-way housing where my dad was not allowed to stay with his wife and his three children. Eventually they were housed in the council flat in Highbury where I was born, and where I grew up.

My dad did not have trouble finding work. He was employed by the Post Office. But my mum was not allowed to use her Jamaican teaching qualification to teach in England. She needed to re-train. So she took in sewing throughout my childhood. But she still nursed her dream of becoming a teacher again.

In England, the fabled Mother Country that they had learned so much about at school in Jamaica, my parents were poor and working class.

They believed that in order to get on in this country they should live quietly and not make a fuss. They should assimilate and be as respectable as they possibly could. Clean the front step every week. Go to church on Sundays. Keep their children well dressed and scrubbed behind the ears.

On one occasion my mum did not have money to buy food for our dinner. None at all. She worried that she might be forced into the humiliation of asking someone, a neighbour perhaps, for a loan. She walked out into the street praying for a solution, and found a one-pound note lying on the pavement. In my mum's eyes that was not a stroke of luck, that was a strategy.

My parents believed that, with no real entitlement to anything, they must accept what this country was willing to give. They were, after all, immigrants. As long as they didn't do anything too unusual that might upset the people of England, then they could get on. My mum was desperate for my dad to lose his accent and stop saying 'nah man' and 'cha' in every sentence. They never discussed Jamaica with anyone. My mum would get embarrassed if she saw a black person drawing attention to themselves. It drew attention to her as well, and she hated that.

My family is fair-skinned. In Jamaica this had had a big effect on my parents' upbringing, because of the class system, inherited from British colonial times, people took the colour of your skin very seriously. My parents had grown up to believe themselves to be of a higher class than any darker-skinned person. This isolated them from other black Caribbeans who came to live here – they wanted nothing to do with them.

My mum once told me how, back in Jamaica, her father would not let her play with children who were darker than her. She said wistfully, 'But I had to, or I would have had no one to play with.' So when she came to England she was pleased to be bringing her children up amongst white children. We would always have lighter-skinned children to play with. I was expected to isolate myself from darker-skinned people too, and it seemed perfectly normal to me that the colour of your skin was one of the most important things about you. White people of course never had to think about it. But if you were not white, well then, how black were you? I accepted all of this as logical. That was how I would be judged.

Light-skinned or not, still we were asked, 'When are you going back to your own country?' 'Why are you here?' 'Why is your food so funny?' 'Why does your hair stick up?' 'Why do you smell?' The message was that our family was foreign and had no right to be here. When a member of the far-right group the National Front waved one of their leaflets in my face and started laughing, I felt I owed *them* some sort of apology.

I wanted them to like me. It would be years before I realised I could be angry with them.

The racism I encountered was rarely violent, or extreme, but it was insidious and ever present and it had a profound effect on me. I hated myself. I was ashamed of my family, and embarrassed that they came from the Caribbean.

In my efforts to be as British as I could be, I was completely indifferent to Jamaica. None of my friends knew anything about the Caribbean. They didn't know where it was, or who lived there, or why. And they had no curiosity about it beyond asking why black people were in this country. It was too foreign and therefore not worth knowing.

As I got older my feeling of outsiderness became more marked, as did the feeling that nothing in my background – my class or my ethnicity – was really worth having. At art college I encountered middle-class people for the first time. Proper middle class – debutantes with ponies, that sort of thing. Keeping those origins of mine a secret became paramount. Few people at my college knew I lived on a council estate. Once, when given a lift home, I got my friends to drop me at the gate of a proper house. I walked up the path waving them off. Then as soon as they were out of view I walked back to my flat.

I got a degree in textile design and worked as a designer for about ten minutes before I realised it was not for me. After that I worked for a brief while as a shop assistant, a dresser at the BBC and the Royal Opera House, and a receptionist at a family-planning clinic.

Then something happened. I was working part-time for a sex-education project for young people in Islington. One day the staff had to take part in a racism awareness course. We were asked to split into two groups, black and white. I walked over to the white side of the room. It was, ironically, where I felt most at home – all my friends, my boyfriend, my flatmates, were white. But my fellow workers had other ideas and I found myself being beckoned over by people on the black side. With some hesitation I crossed the floor. It was a rude awakening. It sent me to bed for a week.

By this time I was scared to call myself a black person. I didn't feel I had the right qualifications. Didn't you have to have grown up in a 'black community'? Didn't you need to go to the Caribbean a lot? Didn't your parents need to be proud of being black? Didn't my friends need to be black? My upbringing was so far removed from all of that, I felt sure I would be found out as an imposter. I was not part of the black experience, surely?

It was a life-changing moment.

Fortunately I had recently enrolled on an afternoon-a-week writing course at the City Lit in London, just as a hobby. Writing came to my rescue. The course had an emphasis on writing about what you know. So, nervously I began to explore what I knew – my family upbringing and background, and my complicated relationship with colour. Thinking about what I knew, and exploring my background with words, began to open it up for me as never before. I soon came to realise that my experience of growing up in this country was part of what it meant to be black. All those agonies over skin shade. Those silences about where we had come from. The shame. The denial. In fact I came to see that every black person's life, no matter what it is, is part of the black experience. Because being black in a majority white country comes with a myriad of complications and contradictions. It was writing that helped me to understand that.

A few months into the course I had the urge to visit Jamaica for the very first time and stay with the family I had never met. I went for Christmas. It was an amazing experience. I discovered a family I had never really known I had. I realised that I meant something to people who lived on the other side of the world. I met my aunt and cousins and saw where my mum grew up. I realised for the first time that I had a background and an ancestry that was fascinating and worth exploring. Not only that, but I had the means to do it – through writing.

I am now happy to be called a black British writer, and the fiction I have written has all been about my Caribbean heritage in some way or another. It is a very rich seam for a writer and it is, quite simply, the reason that I write. Toni Morrison was once asked if she felt constrained by her being seen as a black writer. She replied: '*being a black woman writer is not a shallow place but a rich place to write from. It doesn't limit my imagination; it expands it.*' That is how I feel.

The more I began to delve into my Caribbean heritage the more interesting Britain's Caribbean story became for me. The story of the Caribbean is a white story too and one that goes back a long way. The region was right at the very heart of Europe's early experiments in colonising the world. In the 1500s it was the Spanish who first exploited those newly found islands, displacing the indigenous people. The Dutch, the French and the British came soon after. The island claimed earliest for Britain was Barbados, in 1625. But soon Britain was a major coloniser in the region. A whole string of islands became 'British'. Islands that for a long time were seen as our most lucrative overseas possessions. Sugar was the main crop, as important to Britain then as oil is today. It was planted, harvested and processed by the slave labour of black Africans. That slave trade from West Africa to the Caribbean and the Americas was the largest forced migration in human history. Those islands soon became brutal island-factories helping to fuel and to fund the industrial revolution in Britain. Huge family fortunes were made. Major cities like Bristol, Liverpool and London grew wealthy on the proceeds. The money that slavery in the Caribbean generated was reinvested in Britain's industry and infrastructure. Britain's empire grew as a result.

When British slavery finally ended in 1833, compensation was paid by the British Government. It amounted to twenty million pounds (many billions in today's money). It was paid to the slave owners for the loss of their property. They were seen as the injured party.

But there is more to those Caribbean islands than just the history of slavery. Many white people went, if not in chains, then under duress: indentured servants and poor people from all corners of Britain who were trying to escape hardship at home or to build a new life. Many were press-ganged sailors, or convict labour. There were Sephardic Jews from Iberia, merchants from the Middle East and, later, indentured labourers from India and China. A social mix was created like in no other place on earth. Creole cultures developed with a wide range of skin colours that were elaborately classified (mulatto, quadroon, octoroon and so on) as a divide-and-rule tactic by the British plantocracy. Racial difference and racial value developed into a 'science'. After the end of slavery in the Caribbean the British continued to rule their islands through a policy of racial apartheid right up until they finally left in the nineteen sixties.

But all this happened three thousand miles away from Britain, and as a result it has been possible for it to quietly disappear from British mainstream history. This is the absence, the gap in knowledge, the amnesia of the British that made the black man on the bus such an alien. It is unthinkable that a book on American history could leave out plantation slavery in the southern states. But in British history books the equivalent is the case, or at least the importance of those centuries of British slavery in the Caribbean is underplayed. That British plantation slavery has no lasting legacy for this country is absurd, but it is a claim that is made implicitly by this silence. It was so very long ago, it seems to say, we don't need to dredge it up.

I remember what I was taught at school about Britain in the Caribbean. I had one lesson on the transatlantic slave trade. We looked at illustrations of slaves in ships. But that was all. I learned much more about William Wilberforce and the campaign for the abolition of slavery than anything about the life of a slave. We know more about slavery in the American South than in the British Caribbean. We are familiar with the struggles of African-Americans from the Civil War to the Civil Rights movement. But American slavery was different from Caribbean slavery. In the Caribbean, slaves far outnumbered the white owners, and that mix of isolation, fear and dependency produced very different societies from those of the American South. America's story will not do for us. Our legacy of slavery is unique, and we need to understand what it is.

I wrote a novel, *The Long Song*, set in the time of slavery in the Caribbean, and when I was promoting the book I had numerous media interviews. On two separate occasions the interviewers – bright, university-educated people in each case – admitted to me that they had not known that Britain had used slaves in the Caribbean. Slavery they thought had only been in America. Going around the country doing readings I was surprised at the ignorance of people about where the islands were, or of how many of them there were. Many people I met believed all people from the Caribbean came from Jamaica.

And what of the period after slavery? What about the century of 'racial apartheid' that grew up in the colonial era, the time when my mum and dad learned to know their racial place and to keep themselves separate? The history of the black people of the Caribbean is missing.

Apart from being an exotic holiday destination the islands have now become an irrelevance here. They are no longer wealthy. They are not rich with natural resources. They no longer have the power they enjoyed when some of the most famous families in Britain were there. It is too easy to forget what happened and how it has affected our lives today. But it is as much a part of

British history as the Norman Conquest, or the Tudors.

No one would claim that out of Britain's many stories of empire the Caribbean is the most important. But it is one of the earliest, one of the longest in duration, and certainly one of the most unusual in terms of population mix and the creation of unique societies. In other parts of Britain's old empire, such as India or Africa, we can debate what fading legacy the British have left, whether it is railways, bureaucracies or parliamentary systems. In the Caribbean the legacy is, in one sense, everything. Not just the towns, the cities and the landscape, but the very people themselves; their origins, their ethnic mix, their hybrid cultures, all result from what the British did on those islands before they finally left them. And conversely, Britain growing to become a world power, its attitudes to race, and even how it sees itself today, these things are in no small part the legacy that the British Caribbean has left for modern Britain. '*The very notion of Great Britain's "greatness" is bound up with Empire,*' the cultural theorist, Stuart Hall, once wrote: '*Euro-scepticism and little Englander nationalism could hardly survive if people understood whose sugar flowed through English blood, and rotted English teeth.*'

What this means of course is that I, and my family,

are products of Britain just as much as the white kids I grew up with in Highbury. Given Britain's history in the Caribbean it was almost inevitable that people like my dad and his fellow passengers on the *Windrush* would end up here. They belonged, whether Britain realised it or not. One of the consequences of having an empire, of being a cultural hub, is that the world ultimately comes to you. That's how hubs work.

Britons of Caribbean heritage have been in this country in significant numbers for sixty-five years now. We are three or four generations on from the man on the London bus. Immigration to Britain since the end of the Second World War has been a final, unexpected gift to Britain from its old empire. The benefits that the labour and the enterprise of immigrants, like those from the Caribbean, have brought to Britain are incalculable. Their ideas, their creativity and their ways of life have helped turn this country into a sophisticated multi-culture. This windfall of talent and variety is one of the great unforeseen benefits to Britain.

But there are still countless young Britons today of Afro-Caribbean descent who have as little understanding of their ancestry and have as little evidence of their worth as I did when I was growing up. And there are countless white Britons who are unaware of the histories that bind us together. Britain made the Caribbean that my parents came from. It provided the people – black and white – who make up my ancestry. In return my ancestors, through their forced labour and their enterprise, contributed greatly to the development of modern Britain. My heritage is Britain's story too. It is time to put the Caribbean back where it belongs – in the main narrative of British history.

Introduction to *The Diary*

In this book I have gathered together my short stories. Because short stories are short it is often mistakenly thought that it does not take long to write them. I was once offered a week to write a story by an editor with the words, 'It doesn't have to be long.' But as the famous quote (Pascal? Twain? Goethe? Cicero?) says, 'I'd write you a shorter letter, but I haven't the time'. Short stories can be as consuming as any novel.

This story was one of my first. The central idea came to me in a dream – not the plot but the dilemma.

I first read it aloud at the writing class I was attending at the City Lit. I'd been longing to exorcise the experiences I had of working as a dresser for ballet dancers, and their tutus. At last I could get my own back, I thought. But what I really enjoyed as I read it out was that people laughed. It was much more satisfying than the revenge. And once I'd made them laugh they seemed more open to what I had to say. I have never forgotten that.

The Diary

No, I COULDN'T READ it — not someone else's diary, someone else's secrets...

It beat ironing crotch elastic. Ballet dancers! Crotch elastic is a length of elastic that runs from the back part of a tutu to the front. It holds the bodice down and stops the frilly bit jumping up and whacking the dancer in the face. You can imagine what an inch-wide piece of white elastic would look like after being wrapped round that part of a female's anatomy for two hours of prancing and pirouetting. It was my job to iron it flat. After every performance I had to iron it back into shape. Me. Four years at college, a degree in drama, the talent to become a great actress, and I end up cross-eyed over an ironing board. I used to look out of the window as I ran my iron back and forth, into the windows of the next building. There were people in there sitting at desks. They would sit there all day writing on bits of paper with their heads down. And I was so depressed I'd think, 'That looks like fun – I wish I was in there.' Until one day I said, 'I've got to get out.' And I left – just like that – mid-elastic. To hell with it, I thought, life's too short.

Then Zania, a costume designer, rang me. She'd heard I'd gone AWOL from Covent Garden but she didn't mind. She was desperate for a dresser and some imaginative person had told her I could sew.

'You can sew?' she asked me.

'I have sewn,' I said. Meaning, I had sewn name tags on to my school uniform many years earlier. But I needed the work.

She told me the pay – I thought she meant per hour; she meant per week. But, 'Oh, it's the theatre – just think of the experience,' she said.

I half believed her. There's glamour in being exploited for art.

So I went up to see her at the theatre. The Royal Theatre where many famous people got their first break. Julie Andrews even played there once, or so the rumour had it. I went up to the costume department, which was an extraordinarily grand name for a room no bigger than my bedroom at home, stuffed full of boxes, washing machines, tumble dryers and clothes in various stages of making. There was about a square foot in the middle of the room that you could actually move about in. It was hard to imagine the magnificence that is Julie Andrews in that room.

But Zania said I'd get my name on the programme as a company member. I liked the sound of that – a company member – it sounded egalitarian. I could see myself watching rehearsals, passing comments to the director, who'd pass them on to a grateful cast. Discussing Shakespeare and Pinter in the bar together – the actors, the director, me. An intellectual exercise. I took the job and Zania started me sewing gussets into trousers to make them two sizes bigger.

Then I found out he was in the play. Had she said that before I'd have said yes like a shot – she needn't have gone on about art and the shared experience. I only found out when I was sewing labels into hats one day. She'd given me a list of names and there it was at the top – Paul Riceman. Paul Riceman was great. I'd seen nearly every film he'd been in, except the one about the mass-murdering woman-hater. He had a way of making every part he played humorous. Even when he was a total baddie you ended up rooting for him instead of the good guy. He had beautiful eyes – dark like lychee stones. When he smiled his face crinkled up and his beautiful eyes became two black dashes. He was lovely. I'd spent nights dreaming of meeting him and looking into those eyes. And of him falling in love with my innocence and poverty. Introducing me with gentle, loving paternalism to the life of a famous international actor.

But as it turned out I only got to talk to him once. One afternoon, I was sitting on the floor in the costume department eating a sandwich. It was, unfortunately, one of those sandwiches where you bite one end and the entire filling spurts out the other. I was trying to catch the cheese, pickle and lettuce with my hand and get it into my mouth before it slid to the floor, when I heard a voice.

'Is Zania around?'

I looked up and it was him. I had a mouthful of bread and I could feel Branston pickle sliding down my chin. I swallowed hard and said, 'No,' as alluringly as I could.

He then said, 'Could you tell her I'm looking for her?' and smiled.

I nodded and tried to smile back but I was scared about green lettuce on my teeth so I didn't grin too broadly. He left the doorway and I thought, just my luck: my big chance to wow him with my charms and I look like a two-year-old at lunch.

I thought there would be other opportunities but he was never around when I went to his dressing room to deliver things. Just his presence was there; his comb with five golden hairs trapped around the teeth, his cashmere jacket on the back of the chair, his well-worn pan-stick concealer. And I never got to dress him – he requested a man.

I got to dress Hester Walker. I used to fluff her dresses, clean her shoes, then hold them out to her so she could get in. And she never looked at me, not in the eyes. She'd just order me to get her a sandwich or dry her tights. I kept thinking of Mammy in *Gone with the Wind* – 'Yes, sir, missy, did you say an avocado and prawn sandwich? Coming right up – ha, ha, ha.' But Zania told me I had to keep Hester happy – that I wasn't to upset her because she was prone to throwing wobblies and walking out mid-performance.

I did this for four weeks. Egalitarian? It was just one step away from slavery. The step being that I got to keep my own name. But the saddest thing of all was that I had made no impression on Paul Riceman. I had to admit that after our four weeks together Paul Riceman would have had trouble picking me out in an identity parade.

Anyway, Zania didn't need me any more because the show was running. So I packed my belongings and left. When I got home I realised I had picked up someone else's book by mistake. The hardcover was the same colour as mine but when I opened it, it wasn't *Down and Out in Paris and London*. In fact it wasn't a printed book at all. It was full of handwriting. I turned a few pages and looked at the densely written, tiny script and realised it was someone's diary.

I turned to the front page thinking that some people are stupid enough to put their names in the front of diaries. But there wasn't a name. I turned to the back. Some people are stupid enough to put their names at the back. Written in tiny script at the bottom of the page was 'Paul Riceman' and a date. I was staring at Paul Riceman's diary. And this was not a 'dinner with Zsa Zsa' diary – this was pages and pages of writing, probably straight from the heart.

I didn't know what to do. They didn't teach me this

at college. I thought, I'll take it back, put it down somewhere where he'll find it. But then someone else might find it, someone who'd have no qualms about reading it. They might even sell it to the *News of the World*, or worse, *The Sunday Times*. I could post it to him. But what if it got lost in the post or they opened it at the stage door thinking it might be a bomb, then read it? Or I could just put it in an envelope with Paul Riceman written on it and leave it in the dressing room. But someone might see me − ask me what I'm doing back sneaking round the dressing rooms. I couldn't do that. So I thought, I'll go and give it to him. But he'd look at me and think I'd read it, or worse, that I stole it on purpose. He might call the police, anything!

I thought about it for hours with all the possibilities and problems alternating in my head. Until I decided, 'Oh to hell with it − I'll pretend I never found it.'

I hid it in the top drawer of my chest of drawers. It's hard to hide something from yourself; you try not to be there when you do it, hope you'll forget as you do with Biros and Sellotape. But I couldn't. I kept remembering that that thing was next to my knickers. And a little voice in my head kept saying: 'Read it − read it, stupid.'

I started opening it accidentally, but the writing was

so small I couldn't make anything out unless I really concentrated on it, so I'd close it up again. It sat there for days. And it got harder to resist. It was like knowing you've got a box of chocolates when you've got the munchies real bad. But I couldn't read it. I kept remembering the look on my mum's face after she had 'sneaked a look' at my adolescent journal. And how she gave the book back but kept the secrets. No, I couldn't read it, not someone else's diary – not Paul Riceman's diary.

Then I had an idea. I took the diary out of the drawer and holding it close to my chest I walked down to the library. With my last £5 I bought a card. I went to the photocopying machine, placed the card in the slot, took out the diary and carefully, so nobody else could see the text, I photocopied the entire book. Every single page. I smiled as I watched the pages piling up neatly on the tray. Photocopies, I reasoned, are not the real thing. I could read photocopies. I would still be able to say, with my hand on my heart, that I had never read the diary.

When I got home I hid the real diary, putting it in several different places in the hope that I really wouldn't remember where I finally placed it. And I started to read the photocopies. It took a very long time. Paul's handwriting was small and mean with no loops or flourishes to help. By the time I'd finished I felt like I'd eaten a box of chocolates by myself – soft centres and all. I felt sick. I knew more about Paul Riceman than I did about my own mother. I knew more about him than he would want anyone to know. I knew his secrets, what made him laugh and what made him growl. What turned him on, and off. I knew who he liked, who he hated, who he loved. It was as if the contents of his head had been tipped out into my lap for me to pick through. It was horrible.

I couldn't think about anything else. I couldn't sleep without seeing him. I couldn't eat without thinking of him. I turned on the television and as the picture came into view there he was. Paul Riceman sitting on a sofa in a gaudy set. He was everywhere. I thought I was going mad. But he looked as he always did: an Englishman full of charm and boyish humour, playing with his hair and flirting with the presenter. But if they knew about the afternoon of 21st September, or that January in the Caribbean, they wouldn't sit so close to him.

It was then I decided to burn the diary. Make a bonfire out of it. Put an end to the whole sordid business.

Forget Paul Riceman and get back to my own life.

But just as I was going to turn the television off, I heard him say he was looking for an actress, someone to star with him in his next film. He giggled. 'But the actress I'm looking for,' he said, 'would need a certain something.' I stopped. My finger paused over the button. I took a deep breath and this strange feeling came over me. It started way down in my stomach and gradually rippled up me. It made me sit up straight. My left eyebrow went up on my forehead, my mouth began to smile. I didn't feel so small. It was the strangest sensation and I didn't know what it was. Then that voice said to me, 'You're an actress, and you've got a certain something.'

I picked up the phone and as I dialled the theatre and said, 'Paul Riceman, please,' I realised what the feeling was. It was power.

Introduction to *Deborah*

This story was written for an anthology called *New Writing* 7, which was commissioned by the British Council. The brief was very open – just write a short story. At the time the newspapers were full of discussions about evil children. There had been a horrible murder committed by two minors and the country was rightly shocked. But it made me remember my own childhood.

The story is roughly based on something that I witnessed when I was young girl growing up on a council estate in the early 1960s. All of us kids from the estate used to play outside together from morning until night. We had great freedom to roam. But we also had some very troubling experiences. *Deborah* reminds me of where I came from and also that our lives are too complex for such simple notions as good and evil.

Deborah

DEBORAH LIVED IN MY flats at number forty-six, on the ground floor next to the drying room. It was a long way from where I lived, which was on the same floor but round the bend in the balcony. If I looked out of my bedroom window I could see into Deborah's. When the wind blew, the curtains of her flat usually flew out the top of the open window and fluttered around – knocking against the bricks, billowing up, waving in front of the windows above. As the curtains blew, you could catch a glimpse of all the beds that were squashed into the bedrooms in Deborah's flat. Nobody ever really knew how many there were in Deborah's family. Some said twelve, others said fourteen. And Deborah, when I asked her, said it depended on whether her dad was home.

After our church harvest festival, the vicar would bring Deborah's mum some of the baskets with the fruit and tins of beans and biscuits that we had collected.

'Why don't we get any?' I asked my mum.

'Because they need it and we have it to give,' she would say.

But Deborah always told me, 'In my house, Coca-Cola comes out of the taps, not water.' And I told my mum and asked if we could have that too.

But she said, 'Don't go believing what that girl says. Deborah is a liar.'

Deborah could have a pretty face. Sometimes at school when they made her wash it in the little basins in the toilet, you could clearly see her pale blue eyes with their dark outer ring, and her pink cheeks that could puff up into a smile like a hamster storing nuts. Her teeth were white and small and stuck out in the front because, when no one was looking, she would suck her thumb, even though she was nine like me. And when she spoke her tongue hit her teeth and made her sound like a baby. She had little rings of grey cotton thread through her ears where they were pierced. 'It keeps me holes open,' she told everyone. ' 'Cause I lost me gold earrings.' Her socks always looked the same – grey that once was white – one up, one down, with most of the fabric sliding inside her shoe, revealing the back of her ankle and heel which were always crusted with black dirt. Her left shoe had a buckle and strap that worked, but the right one flapped open and when she ran fast she had to hop to keep it on. She wore dresses like all the girls did, but Deborah's waistband was always too high and the first two buttons on the back of her dress never did up. And Deborah smelt. She smelt of behind my bed where there were speckles of black on the wall. She smelt of milk going off and old shoe-bags in the cloakroom at school and the bottom of the bin after you'd tipped the contents down the shute.

Deborah came to my front door nearly every day. 'Can Fern come out to play?' she'd ask.

Sometimes my mum would look down at her and say, 'She can't come out today, she's got a cold.'

At which Deborah would say, 'Well let us come in then.'

And my mum would say, 'No, she's ill.'

Deborah would put her hands on her hips. 'Let her come to the door then.'

'No! Fern is not well. You understand me?' Mum would then have to shut the door.

But Deborah would lift up the letter box and shout down the hall, 'Fern, are you coming out to play?'

While my mum tutted, 'The cheek of that girl!'

There was a woman who lived upstairs, on the first balcony, over the pram sheds. Her name was Mrs Wheeler. She had hair that looked like yellow candyfloss, whipped up and piled on top of her head in a style called a bird's nest. She stank of perfume, and we'd hold our noses when she went by and say, 'Poo, I can still smell it,' after she'd been gone for ages. She used to come on to her balcony and ask one of us kids to go on an errand to the shops for her. She was always doing that, and someone would go and buy her a tin of peas or some potatoes. When you brought them back she'd give you sixpence for going. But she never let Deborah go for her.

'Not you,' she'd say when Deborah would step forward with a grin on her face. 'I've given you money before and I never see nothing for it.'

Deborah would stop smiling and shout back at her. She'd shout, 'Shut up, you silly old cow! Go and get it yourself, you lazy old bag.'

I was always shocked at Deborah's cheek to grown-ups. But it made me giggle and we'd all laugh in the porch. Except no one could earn a sixpence after that.

Deborah cheated in games. She stuck the ball down her knickers in, 'Queenie-eye, Queenie-eye, who's got the ball?' She always moved in 'Peep behind the curtain', and would push you hard and say, 'No I never,' if you complained that she did. When we played the game where you take a step forward if the letter called out is in your name, she always won. Because she said she had loads of middle names that had all the zeds and exes that no one else had. But she made them up – the Zazas and Lexys. Everybody knew it because they weren't even real names. And when we played shows in the porch with everyone standing up in turn and singing *Bachelor Boy* or *How Much Is That Doggie In The Window*, Deborah, on her go, would just get up and show everybody her knickers because she couldn't sing and didn't know any songs.

But she was really good for some things. She could make herself go all floppy like a rag doll. So on Guy Fawkes night we made her the guy. We put one of those cardboard masks, that you buy from the sweetshop, over her face. Then we sat her outside the gate of the flats and waited for people to come past.

'Penny for the guy,' we said.

And everyone looked at us impressed. 'That's a good

guy,' they'd say, then give us money for Deborah.

But then this man insisted on sticking the money into the guy's mouth. And Deborah had to suck a threepenny bit.

She jumped up spitting and screaming, 'I've swallowed thousands of germs. I'm gonna die.'

She wouldn't do it any more after that. 'You do it now, Fern,' she said. But no one could get as floppy as Deborah.

She could get your ball back from anywhere. If someone hit it over the wall into the gardens of the houses, Deborah would take a run at the wall, scamper over it and disappear for a few minutes. Then the ball would be thrown back and Deborah would climb back after it. And if someone shouted, 'Oihh you,' Deborah would stick her two fingers up at them. She could go over railings, walk along walls. She could jump all ten of a flight of steps without having to hold the banister. She just threw herself off, landing on her hands and knees. Scraped hands and bloody knees never bothered Deborah. 'It don't hurt me. Nothing hurts me,' she'd say. And she'd show you her scabs if she liked you.

I didn't really want to play at Deborah's – her house smelt. And Deborah's mum's stockings hung down from her knees, and her legs were fat and white and had blue lumpy lines all over them. She wore her slippers in the street and was always shouting. We could hear her in our flat even when the telly was on.

'There goes that woman again,' my mum would say.

But that day Deborah said, 'I wanna show you something,' and I hoped it was the tap where the Cola comes out.

Kenny followed us. He was always doing that.

'What you doing – where you going?' he asked us. He walked two feet behind me and Deborah with his hands in his pockets, kicking at imaginary stones.

'Get lost,' Deborah told him.

But he just looked around then said, 'Where you going – what you doing?' and carried on following.

Kenny was much younger than me and Deborah; that's why he followed us. His mum lived on the third floor and his dad rode a motorbike at weekends. Kenny was a little kid who wore short trousers and was useless at throwing a ball – he'd aim it forward and it would go behind him. He wore glasses that had a grubby pink plaster over one of the lenses because he had a lazy eye. And he was ginger and cried if you called him carrot.

'Let us come?' he said. So we let him because he

didn't have anyone else to play with.

There was no one else in at Deborah's. She took us into her bedroom – the room with loads of beds. There were clothes everywhere. Shoes, knickers and socks where pillows should be. Dresses and trousers all over the beds, hanging off and spilling on to the floor. There was a coat on a hanger that was hanging from the curtain rail – big and dark in the window like a stranger you shouldn't talk to. The curtain was orange and ripped at the bottom with a safety pin through the hole to keep it together. The wallpaper was green – little green flowers all over the room. And there were black footprints up high on the wall. The light socket in the centre of the ceiling didn't have a bulb in it, but had lots of black flex and leads attached instead. And the flex and leads were strung over the room like a Christmas decoration of spiders' legs.

'Are you going to show us the Coca-Cola tap?' I asked her.

'It's not working,' she said. 'Look, I've got something else to show you.' She pointed to the wall over a bed. Just above where the pillow should have been there was a little picture torn out of a magazine with jagged edges up one side, stuck on the wall with Sellotape. It was of

Pinky and Perky. Two pink puppet pigs dressed as if they were going away on holiday, in sunglasses and flowery shirts.

'That's mine,' Deborah said. She jumped on the bed and pointed, 'That's Pinky and that's Perky.'

Kenny started to laugh. 'Is that all you've got?' he said looking around.

'Let's see the tap anyway,' I asked her again.

But Deborah said, 'Do you want to see my bum?' She lifted up her dress and pulled her knickers down.

Kenny put his hand over his mouth, 'Oh you're dirty.' He began to giggle but went up close and put his head right next to it.

'Let's see your bum, Fern,' Deborah said, as she pulled her knickers back up.

'No.'

'I'll show you mine,' Kenny said. He turned round, pulled down his trousers and pushed out his bottom. It had freckles on it. Then he pulled his trousers up again quickly, laughing.

Deborah stuck out her bum again, holding down her knickers and twisting round like she was dancing.

So I showed them mine. And they were quiet for a second as they looked at it. Until we all began to laugh.

Kenny jumped on the bed and started jumping up and down.

'Let's see Kenny's again,' Deborah said and she grabbed at Kenny's trousers. But he held on to them. Deborah pulled hard and they came down. And Kenny pulled them up again.

'Let's see yours again, Fern,' Deborah said.

But I said, 'No.'

'Oh, go on – I showed you mine.' She got on the bed and began jumping with Kenny.

'Let's play something else,' I said. 'Haven't you got any games?'

Deborah jumped off the bed and landed right on me, her face next to mine. 'Fern, do you know that milk comes out of women's tits when she has a baby?'

Kenny was still jumping – getting higher and higher, waving his arms in the air.

'Everybody knows that,' I said.

'You know how they get it to come out?' Deborah carried on.

Kenny started singing, 'Tits and bum, tits and bum,' in time to his jumping.

I didn't answer her. But she said, 'You have to have your nipples pierced with a pin.'

I put my arms across me and screamed with horror, 'Do ya,' and decided never to have a baby.

'Yeah my sister's had it done. How else d'you think it comes out? They put a pin in it and the milk comes out.' Then Deborah put her warm hand right over my chest with her fingers spread out and her palm right over my nipple. She breathed bubble-gum breath into my face and said, 'Shall I show ya?'

Kenny had jumped so high that his arms hit the electric leads that were coming out of the light socket. The light socket pulled out of the ceiling and sent down a shower of plaster and dust over the bed and clothes. In a second things were crashing down everywhere. A light smashed on to the floor and the bulb broke and made a tinkling sound. Something else I couldn't see went thud. We just watched it happen like in a film when a ghost is about. In the end there were just two metal pointy wires coming from a hole in the ceiling and the black flexes and leads were all over the room.

'Kenny, look what you've done,' I shouted.

And Kenny said, 'I never did nothing... I never touched nothing... I never... never did nothing.' But his face screwed up like he was going to cry.

'You better get your mum to fix it, Deborah,' I told her.

Deborah started to shake. She stood in front of me with her legs shivering and her hands trembling like she was cold from coming out of the swimming pool.

'We'll tell her Kenny did it. It wasn't you. Or get your dad – he'll fix it,' I said.

Deborah started to scream, 'No! No! No!' She was looking round her and crying, 'No! No!' She held her hands between her legs, jiggling up and down and screaming, 'No! No!'

Kenny started to giggle at her.

'It's all right, your mum'll fix it,' I told her. But she threw herself on the floor – right at my feet. She laid flat for a second then she wriggled like an insect under the bed. Kenny knelt down to see where she had gone.

'She's crying under the bed,' he said and started to laugh. 'She's a scaredy cat. She's gone under the bed.'

I knelt down and looked. She was squashed against the wall, shaking, with her thumb in her mouth, making little whimpering sounds like a dog.

'Deborah. Come out or I'm going home,' I told her. But she wouldn't move. 'I'm going home,' I shouted.

And I left. I left the room with the plaster and the

dust and the black electric leads like spiders' legs. And I left Deborah under the bed with Kenny in his short grey trousers on his knees pointing at her and saying, 'She's a scaredy cat. She's under the bed and she's crying. She's a cry baby.'

It wasn't until much later that day that I saw Kenny and Deborah again. I was playing two balls up against the wall. It was the farthest I'd ever got before dropping the ball but there was no one around to see. I was on to 'one two three and twisties'. Then I saw Kenny coming out of the drying room and I dropped a ball. He didn't have any clothes on. Nothing. No shoes, no socks, no short grey trousers. He didn't even have his glasses on. He was completely bare. I could see his willie. Dangling between his legs like a little slug – bouncing up and down as he ran from the drying room door. It made me laugh but I put my hand over my mouth so he wouldn't see.

I watched him run along the balcony, his mouth open as if he was screaming but with no sound coming out. He started to move backwards then forwards, left, right – as if he didn't know which way to go. And as he ran his willie kept bobbing up and down. Then Kenny was crying. He saw me and held his arms out to me like a baby, running towards me, wanting to be picked up. And as he got closer I could see that all over his white skin were red slashes. As he got closer I could see that some of them were bleeding – oozing blood. Some of them were raised, some were raw, some of them had blood coming from them in long dribbles. He was striped with them. Over his legs and arms and chest and face. And his eye, the lazy one, was roaming around in its socket – slowly moving from one side to the other.

I didn't want to touch him – I wrapped my arms around me and stepped back as he came close. That's when I saw Deborah coming out of the drying room with a grin on her face, and in her hand she was holding a black lead – like a spider's leg but one with spikey metal ends.

'Go to your mum, Kenny,' I told him. I pointed the way.

He turned round and ran towards the porch. I followed him up the flights of stairs. I followed behind him, listening to him crying and watching his white bottom – slashed and raw pink – slipping from side to side as he lifted his leg up each step.

His mum screamed. Everyone wanted to know where Deborah was. Kenny's dad wanted to know.

Neighbours who stood at open doors wanted to know. Mrs Wheeler from her balcony wanted to know. My mum wanted to know.

'Where is she, Fern? When did you last see her? She whipped that little boy. Where is that evil girl?'

And the shouting started outside Deborah's flat.

Kenny's dad roaring and Deborah's mum yelling, 'If it was her I'll kill her – when I get hold of her I'll kill her.'

The police were called and mingled with everyone who'd come to stare. And Kenny was taken away in an ambulance.

It was me who found her. She was sitting in the top porch, round the block, where we hardly ever go except when we don't want to be found in hide-and-seek. She was sitting in the corner, humming, with her knees up and her cardigan pulled up over her head and down in front of her face. She was sucking her thumb and rocking gently backwards and forwards. And coming out from between her legs was a small trickle of piss that crept slowly along the ground.

Introduction to
That Polite Way That English People Have

This story was written to be read aloud – to be performed at the Southbank Centre in London. The brief was to write a piece centred around the idea of either hot or cold. At the time I was in the very early stages of writing my novel SMALL ISLAND, which looked at the immigration of people from Jamaica to Britain. I didn't really want to break off from that completely. So I thought I could use the idea to explore immigration from a hot country to a cold one. Perfect.

I took the inspiration from a story my mum had told me about the ship journey she made to England from Jamaica in 1948. It was my first outing with the character of Hortense, who would later go on to be a main character in SMALL ISLAND. I wrote the story in the first person. And I soon realised that I would have to perform the story with a Jamaican accent.

My mum was in the audience when I read it out. Afterwards she came to me and asked, 'Where you learn to speak like that?'

I said, 'From you.'

At which she looked at me incredulously and said, 'But I don't speak like that.'

My mum spent years trying to rid herself of her Jamaican accent. And please don't tell her, but she never did.

That Polite Way That English People Have

I WAS SURE MY coat would be the finest coat in England. Oh, everyone would stare – everyone would admire my long black coat and my black hat with its netting trim set at an angle on my head. There, they would say, there is high-class woman from Jamaica. She is a woman who has one of the finest coats.

I bought my coat from my employer, who had only just returned from England after settling her two sons into a boarding school in a place called Dover.

'Blossom,' she said, in that polite way that English people have, 'you will need a coat in England and I have a coat that you may purchase.'

It cost me a great deal of money but Mrs Roberts informed me that since the war the cost of coats in

England had become very high and that this coat I was purchasing from her was the best quality money could buy. I would have, she assured me, no regrets.

I was travelling to England to train as a nurse. And as I would be arriving in England in the month of November, a coat, I felt, would be necessary for keeping out the cold. It was very amusing that the day I purchased the coat from Mrs Roberts was one of the hottest days I had ever encountered in all my living. Mrs Roberts allowed me into her bedroom to view the coat in her dressing-table mirror. And there was I on the hottest day God had ever sent wrapping myself in this thick woollen coat. My employer assured me that it fitted and suited me as if it had been made for I alone. I did not keep on the coat very long because the day was too hot.

Later that afternoon I was carrying eggs home for Mamma and as I walked from the shop one of the eggs slipped from the bag and landed on the road. I was surprised to see that as it hit the hot ground the egg started to cook. I had no chance to bend and scoop it back into the shell. All I could do was watch it turn white.

Mamma had shouted at me, as I was afraid she would.

But I did not pay it any mind. 'Mamma,' I said, 'when I get to England I will send you money enough to drop as many eggs as you so desire.'

But Mamma was not as convinced as I that travelling to England was the best thing that I could do to secure a good future for myself. She said that leaving Jamaica because the weather was too hot was no reason at all. But I told her that was only something that was in the back of my mind. It was true the weather was too hot for me and I could no longer stand the hurricanes that swept the island and rid us of all the food from the trees. It was true that I trembled in my bed when the earth moved under my feet and flung our pictures from the walls. But that was not why I was going to England. I was going to train as a nurse. Mamma said I could train as a nurse in Jamaica, that I did not have to go half way round the world to wear a fine starched uniform. But I told her I was going for better opportunity. 'Mamma,' I said, 'I will live in a nice house with a garden smelling of sweet roses. And I will take tea in the finest teahouses in London where they drink from china cups and eat cake by slicing it with the side of a fork.'

Mamma thought I was spending too much money on my passage. But I had worked hard for that money

– from the age of sixteen I was a nanny to three English children. And I saved. Every week a small portion of my wage was placed in the Building Society so that one day I could travel to England. Mamma thought I could have gone on the *SS Windrush* ship with the £28 and 10 shilling passage. I laughed.

'Mamma,' I said, 'that ship was for men.' Could she see me on a ship with nowhere to lie down or place my things? Could she see me on a troop ship amongst all those men with their cards and gambling and carrying on? 'No Mamma,' I told her, 'I will travel to England in style.' But she did not understand. All she could see was the money she said I had wasted. Mamma was a country girl. She was not what English people would call refined. She had not been as educated as I. She had not had the benefit of living for almost ten years in the household of one of the foremost English families in Jamaica. She had not seen how high life can be.

Which is why Mamma kept coming to me with food to pack into the trunk I was taking with me on my journey. She told me that she had heard from a woman at her church that there was no food in England. 'Blossom,' she told me, 'English people are starving – they are still on rations from the war.' And she came to me with her arms full of onions, sugar, rice, guava, limes, mango, paw paw and enough ginger for everyone I would meet. 'Mamma,' I had to say, 'stop! Where am I to put all my warm clothes, my pictures from home – where am I to put my coat?' But still she tried to make me take some eggs. 'Mamma,' I told her, 'I would never get to England with the eggs unbroken.'

Mamma wanted to come to see me off. 'Let me come to the dock with you, Blossom,' she said. 'Help you carry your things.' But I told her she was too old to travel so far. The dock was in Ocho Rios and she was in Kingston. And it was too hot. She said the heat did not bother her. 'But the noise and the crowds, Mamma, the noise and the crowds!' No, we said goodbye in the room Mamma and I had shared for the past two years. I went to the ship on my own – a first-class passenger amongst English travellers.

My trunk was carried on to the ship by a man who was rough and uncouth. He made me glad to be leaving the island. He sucked his teeth as he showed me to my cabin. And as he threw my trunk down he started to scratch himself, on his backside, on his head. Well, it was so hot in the room that I fanned my face a little with the back of my hand. And this man looked at me, leaned his breath into my face and said, 'Remember you're a nigger.' But I paid him no mind. That class of people are so jealous that the high class of us have a chance to better ourselves in England while they are left in the sun scratching out a living and waiting for the pumpkins to grow after the hurricane.

I had the luxury of having a cabin for two all to myself. Two beds – one on top of the other – a washbasin, a lavatory, a light that worked with a flick of a switch and a round window that looked over the sea. The ship was so big, bigger than I had seen in my mind's eye. I had thought of toy boats with paper sails and little wooden stick masts – boats I used to make and play with on the river when I was a girl. But this gigantic metal ship looked too heavy to stay afloat on something as unsteady as water. And the wooden deck seemed to stretch as far as I could see. They were loading up the hold with bananas, oranges, lemons, and crates and crates of I know not what. But the passengers? Oh, they were mostly English people returning from a holiday or going to England to visit a relative or to do a little business. And as they came on board they said 'Good day' and 'Good morning' in that polite way that English people have.

I wished at that moment that there was someone there to see me on this ship: a first-class passenger among English people. Someone to say there is Blossom Hunter, a high-class woman waiting to voyage on an adventure to the Mother Country. As I walked on the deck I ran my hand along the cool of the rail and thought I saw Mamma. Down on the dock. I thought I saw her looking up at the ship. Standing in her yellow floral print dress with her white church hat sitting low on her head. I raised my hand to shield my eyes against the sun and looked again. But there was no one there.

It was then that a man came up and stood beside me. He said, 'Excuse me,' in that polite way. 'Excuse me, miss, but have you lost something?' And I looked up into the face of the most handsome English gentleman I had ever seen. His jaw was square and firm. His slim moustache traced his top lip and his dark hair that was parted to one side was slicked down like a movie star. I had to catch my breath. He spoke again in that deep English way, 'I am sorry, did I startle you?'

I did not know what to say. 'Oh no, sir,' I said. 'I am not startled. It was just that I thought I may have seen somebody who was familiar to me on the dock side.'

He looked out to see where I was looking and I had to tell him, 'But I think I was mistaken.'

He had enjoyed a holiday in Jamaica and was now returning home, he told me. He asked me if I was travelling to England and whether I was travelling alone. I nodded my head politely. Oh, he looked like a doctor or a lawyer or the manager of a good bank. As he left he held out his hand for me to shake, 'My name is Philip Keyes. May I have the pleasure of your acquaintance?'

'Of course you may,' I said and shook his hand.

He asked, 'May I ask your name?'

It was at that point, as he waited for my reply, that I decided Blossom was not a name to carry to England. Blossom was a name that was yelled from doorways in the hot sun. Women called Blossom fanned themselves with banana leaves and drank coconut milk straight from the nut. No, I decided I would use my real name. The name I was christened with – a name which would allow me to blend with teatime and croquet on the lawn.

'Hortense,' I told him, 'My name is Hortense Hunter.'

'Well, Hortense,' this proper English gentleman said,

'I have done a lot of travelling in my time so if you have any problems please do not hesitate to ask my advice.' He bowed his head to me as he said, 'I hope we will meet again at dinner.'

I watched him walk tall and erect along the smooth deck. And I began to feel a breeze ruffle through my dress, caressing and cooling me. But then I thought I saw Mamma again. As the ship slowly moved away from the dockside I thought I saw her. Half hidden behind a truck. Her yellow dress, her white hat. As the dock drifted backwards I thought I saw her step out from behind the truck, raise her arms into the air and call, 'Blossom, Blossom.' But it could not have been Mamma. It was too far and too hot for Mamma to come.

That night everyone got dressed up in their fine clothes and went to dinner. The room was full of chatter. English chatter, about the weather, the ship, the food. Everywhere was 'How do you do?' and 'Please come and join us' and 'Waiter, waiter, do you have tea?' Women with their hair neatly waved and sparkling jewels round their neck. Men with crisp white shirts and bow ties. I had on my best dress, a dress Mamma had made me for a house party I had attended a few years earlier. I brightened up this green dress with a strip of yellow satin ribbon across the low neckline and over the puffed sleeves. And I finished the whole look off with a small piece of ribbon as a bow in my hair. I thought to myself, Hortense, you will need more than this one party dress if every night is like this in England.

The room was bright and shining with white tablecloths and silver knives and forks and crystal glasses at every place. And as I walked in the English gentleman, Mr Keyes, rose from his seat and said, 'Miss Hunter, would you do me the honour of joining me?' I felt like a million dollars. I hoped I did not blush as I slipped into the seat beside him. I nodded and said 'Good day' to everyone sitting at our table, which was the polite thing to do. And as we ate plates and plates of food brought to us by waiters in clean white jackets, Philip, as he asked me to call him, enquired as to why I was travelling to England.

'I will be training as a nurse,' I told him. And he asked me if I had ever been to England before. 'Oh no,' I said, 'but I know a lot about England because I have read about it in books.' This seemed to amuse him. So I told him that I was looking forward to seeing daffodils when I got to England. A host of golden daffodils swaying bright yellow in the breeze in one of the parks – maybe Hyde Park or Regent's Park or Richmond Park. He smiled – he could see I knew about England. And cricket, I told him. I wanted to see the cricket at Lord's and ask a London policeman the time and ride a red bus around Trafalgar Square. I was going to continue to tell him all the other things I would be doing but he held up his hand and said, 'Yes, you certainly know about England, Hortense.'

Then this woman – a Jamaican woman as black as night – sat down at our table. She looked so dressed up with her ribbons and lace, trying to look high class. But I could tell she was rough. Even though she said 'Good evening' and 'How do you do?' to everyone, I could tell. She called herself Petal. 'Good evening, my name is Petal,' she said. But when she ate she talked with her mouth open, showing everyone her food, and she wiped her napkin across her face instead of just dabbing it at the corners of her mouth like English people do.

Then she leaned across to me. 'You going to England?' I tried to ignore her but she hissed at me, 'Sister?' And I had to inform her and Philip and everyone else at the table that I was most certainly not her sister. But she paid me no mind. 'Where you from?' she said to me. I tried to ignore her again by listening very closely to an interesting conversation about lilac trees being carried out by Philip and two women who were returning home to Northamptonshire. But this Jamaican woman knocked my arm in an uncouth manner and said, 'Where you from?' So I told her St Mary just to shut her up, and she said loudly, 'Oh, you a country girl.' I laid down my napkin and informed her that I had lived for ten years in the household of one of the foremost English families in Kingston. But this woman just looked in my face then held her head back and laughed.

I was pleased when Philip asked me if I would like to dance with him. I answered this handsome English gentleman, 'Oh no, Philip, thank you very much but I am a little too tired to dance at this time.' I had to refuse because I had not learned to dance in that two-by-two way that English people do. I was happy that I could turn away from this Petal woman and show her that I had better friends. But still the evening was spoiled by her. She kept shouting at everyone to call her Petal and laughing loudly in a rude manner and dancing around the floor wiggling her hips.

I was very tired so I left at ten. As I got up to go

Philip said, 'Hortense, do me the honour of letting me walk you to your cabin?' And I saw this Petal's mouth drop open as she watched me walk out on the arm of this fine English man.

As Philip left me at my cabin door he asked, 'Would you like a night cap?' I laughed a little then thanked him and told him that I did not usually wear anything on my head when I slept. We said good night and I tucked myself into my happy bed and dreamed of life in England.

I did not see Philip for the whole of the next day, but I did not pay it any mind. I went about the ship. I watched people playing with quoits, throwing the hoops on to pegs, and laughing as they landed several yards away. I sat on the reclining chairs that were provided in the shade and watched young people splashing, jumping and screeching in the swimming pool. And as I walked along the deck, smiling at the people I met, I saw a woman I thought I knew from Jamaica. She was a friend of Mrs Roberts, my employer. An English woman who had once told me that I was the best nanny on the whole of the island. And there was she walking along the deck with her small daughter. I was sure she would remember me so I said, 'Good day, I believe we may have met in Kingston.' But she walked straight past me and I realised then that I may have been mistaken. I napped in my room after that. I lay on my bed with the sea breeze cooling me and watched the sea through the window gently rise and fall, rise and fall.

It was not until the evening that I next saw Philip Keyes. He walked into the dining room and there on his arm, squeezing and hugging him up, was Petal. She looked so pleased with herself, swishing her chiffon scarf across her bare shoulders. And as she sat down Philip gently pushed the chair in for her as he had done for me the night before. This Petal clicked her fingers for the waiter and kept giggling and whispering into Philip's ear. And he offered her cigarettes from a silver case and as she smoked them she blew the smoke out over everyone who was sitting at her table. I could see the other English people looking at her from the corner of their eyes. They were not used to someone as low class as she sitting right next to them – amongst them – like she was as good as them. And I saw them thinking, what can a man like him be doing with that sort of woman? All I could think was she had put some sort of spell on him. Philip bowed his head to me when he saw me. But this time I just turned away. I got up and went to my room because I was feeling a little hot.

By the time we got to England it was cold. My skin rose with goose bumps and I shivered on the deck. I was glad to be leaving the ship. For ten days we had been sailing and I was tired of moving up and down, up and down. I longed to place my feet on firm English soil.

And I was pleased that I would no longer have to spend my days avoiding Mr Philip Keyes with his slicked-down hair and Petal clinging on to his arm. Every time that woman saw me she would run to me asking me questions about myself. 'Where will you be living in London, Hortense? Let me get the address,' she said, as if I would want to be friendly with a woman like her once I was in England amongst all those English people. I told her that I had not yet decided which hospital to present myself at when I got to London. 'Oh, Hortense,' she said, 'you should know where you are going to stay. It will be difficult for you.' I informed her firmly that I would be staying at the lodgings that were supplied for trainee nurses once I had presented myself at the hospital. She started to shake her head, 'No, no, Hortense, listen.' Then she said that I should go with her when I left the ship. She told me she had a sister with a room – just a room, mind – in a place called Notting Hill. 'Stay if only for a few nights, Hortense,' she said, 'until you know more about England.' I thought to myself let her mind her business. As if I would stay with a woman like her. No. I just walked away.

There was excitement all around the ship as we sailed into England. But it was very dark and I was a little disappointed that I could not make out Buckingham Palace and Piccadilly Circus as we manoeuvred into the dock. I went to my trunk. I folded all my summer dresses and placed them in beside the mangoes and the paw paw. And I carefully took out my coat. I said to myself, as I slid my arms into this warm garment and did up the buttons one by one, I am not one of those people who comes to England unprepared. I will not shiver in the street in my flimsy summer clothes. Then I took my hat and placed it on my head at just a little angle.

Everyone was out on deck chatting in that polite way that English people have. We all stood in our coats looking to the dockside and some people waved at I don't know what. And I wished Mamma could have been there to see me arrive. Mamma standing on the dockside in her yellow floral print dress with her white church hat sitting low on her head.

But there was Petal, hugging up and kissing Philip Keyes as everyone tried politely not to stare. When she saw me she came over and stood beside me. She looked at me, up and down, up and down. Then she started to shake her head. She said, 'Where did you get that coat?' I wrapped my coat around me a little more – the finest coat in England – and informed her that I had purchased it from my English employer.

'But this is an ugly coat,' Petal whispered to me. So I told her that I had paid a great deal of money for this coat and that my employer had assured me that this was one of the finest quality coats money could buy. But this Petal just looked in my face then held her head back and laughed. 'Your employer has sold you a very old-fashioned coat,' she told me. She ran her black fingers over the fabric; she twisted a button and flicked at the collar.

'Hortense,' she said, 'the English woman rob you. There is nothing fine about this coat.'

Introduction to
Loose Change

I am the daughter of immigrants. England was often a difficult place for my parents. But not everyone was unfriendly. My mum once cried in a stranger's face when he offered her a sandwich because he knew she was hungry. Growing up I was acutely aware of how any act of kindness can mean so much in a hostile land.

This story is not about immigrants but about refugees. People forced to flee their own country for whatever reason and throw themselves on the mercy of another nation. I wrote it after reading too many accounts in the press which seemed to blame the refugees for their plight.

But how many of us would make gestures of kindness if it meant that our comfortable lives would be affected? If truly tested, how would we react?

Loose Change

I AM NOT IN the habit of making friends with strangers. I'm a Londoner. Not even little grey-haired old ladies passing comment on the weather can shame a response from me. I'm a Londoner – aloof sweats from my pores. But I was in a bit of a predicament; my period was two days early and I was caught unprepared.

I'd just gone into the National Portrait Gallery to get out of the cold. It had begun to feel, as I'd walked through the bleak streets, like acid was being thrown at my exposed skin. My fingers were numb searching in my purse for change for the tampon machine; I barely felt the pull of the zip. But I didn't have any coins.

I was forced to ask in a loud voice in this small lavatory. 'Has anyone got three twenty-pence pieces?'

Everyone seemed to leave the place at once – all of them Londoners I was sure of it. Only she was left – fixing her hair in the mirror.

'Do you have change?'

She turned round slowly as I held out a ten pound note. She had the most spectacular eyebrows. I could see the lines of black hair, like magnetised iron fillings, tumbling across her eyes and almost joining above her nose. I must have been staring hard to recall them so clearly now. She had wide black eyes and a round face with such a solid jawline that she looked to have taken a gentle whack from Tom and Jerry's cartoon frying pan. She dug into the pocket of her jacket and pulled out a bulging handful of money. It was coppers mostly. Some of it tinkled on to the floor. But she had change: too much – I didn't want a bag full of the stuff myself.

'Have you a five-pound note as well?' I asked.

She dropped the coins on to the basin area, spreading them out into the soapy puddles of water that were lying there. Then she said, 'You look?' She had an accent but I couldn't tell then where it was from; I thought maybe Spain.

'Is this all you've got?' I asked. She nodded. 'Well

look, let me just take this now...' I picked three coins out of the pile. 'Then I'll get some change in the shop and pay them back to you.' Her gaze was as keen as a cat with string. 'Do you understand – only I don't want all those coins?'

'Yes,' she said softly.

I was grateful. I took the money. But when I emerged from the cubicle, the girl and her handful of change were gone.

I found her again, staring at the portrait of Darcey Bussell. She was inclining her head from one side to the other as if the painting were a dress she might soon try on for size.

I approached her about the money but she just said, 'This is good picture.'

Was it my explanation left dangling or the fact that she liked the dreadful painting that caused my mouth to gape?

'Really, you like it?' I said.

'She doesn't look real. It looks like...' Her eyelids fluttered sleepily as she searched for the right word. 'A dream.'

That particular picture always reminded me of the doodles girls drew in their rough books at school.

'You don't like?' she asked.

I shrugged.

'You show me one you like,' she said.

As I mentioned before, I'm not in the habit of making friends with strangers, but there was something about this girl. Her eyes were encircled with dark shadows so that even when she smiled – introducing herself cheerfully as Laylor – they remained as mournful as a glum kid at a party. I took this fraternisation as defeat but I had to introduce her to a better portrait.

Alan Bennett with his mysterious little brown bag didn't impress her at all. She preferred the photograph of David Beckham. Germaine Greer made her top lip curl and as for A.S. Byatt, she laughed out loud. 'This is child make this?'

We were almost creating a scene. Laylor couldn't keep her voice down and people were beginning to watch us. I wanted to be released from my obligation.

'Look, let me buy us both a cup of tea,' I said. 'Then I can give you back your money.'

She brought out her handful of change again as we sat down at a table – eagerly passing it across for me to take some for the tea.

'No, I'll get this,' I said.

Her money jangled like a win on a slot machine as she tipped it back into her pocket. When I got back with the teas, I pushed over the twenty-pences I owed her. She began playing with them on the tabletop — pushing one around the other two in a figure of eight. Suddenly she leant towards me as if there were a conspiracy between us and said, 'I like art.' With that announcement a light briefly came on in those dull eyes to suggest that she was no more than eighteen. A student, perhaps.

'Where are you from?' I asked.

'Uzbekistan,' she said.

Was that the Balkans? I wasn't sure. 'Where is that?'

She licked her finger, then with great concentration drew an outline on to the tabletop. 'This is Uzbekistan,' she said. She licked her finger again to carefully plop a wet dot on to the map saying, 'And I come from here — Tashkent.'

'And where is all this?' I said, indicating the area around the little map with its slowly evaporating borders and town. She screwed up her face as if to say 'nowhere'.

'Are you on holiday?' I asked.

She nodded.

'How long are you here for?'

Leaning her elbows on the table she took a sip of her tea. 'Ehh, it is bitter!' she shouted.

'Put some sugar in it,' I said, pushing the sugar sachets toward her.

She was reluctant. 'Is for free?' she asked.

'Yes, take one.'

The sugar spilled as she clumsily opened the packet. I laughed it off but she, with the focus of a prayer, put her cup up to the edge of the table and swept the sugar into it with the side of her hand. The rest of the detritus that was on the tabletop fell into the tea as well. Some crumbs, a tiny scrap of paper and a curly black hair floated on the surface of her drink. I felt sick as she put the cup back to her mouth.

'Pour that one away, I'll get you another one.'

Just as I said that a young boy arrived at our table and stood legs astride before her. He pushed down the hood on his padded coat. His head was curious – flat as a cardboard cut-out – with hair stuck to his sweaty forehead in black curlicues. And his face was as doggedly determined as two fists raised. They began talking in whatever language it was they spoke. Laylor's tone was pleading; the boy's aggrieved. Laylor took the money from her pocket and held it up to him. She slapped his hand away when he tried to wrest all the coins from her palm. Then, as abruptly as he had appeared, he left. Laylor called something after him. Everyone turned to stare at her, except the boy who just carried on.

'Who was that?'

With the teacup resting on her lip, she said, 'My brother. He want to know where we sleep tonight.'

'Oh yes, where's that?' I was rummaging through the contents of my bag for a tissue, so it was casually asked.

'It's square we have slept before.'

'Which hotel is it?' I thought of the Russell Hotel, that was on a square – uniformed attendants, bed-turning-down facilities, old-world style.

She was picking the curly black hair off her tongue when she said, 'No hotel, just the square.'

It was then I began to notice things I had not seen before… dirt under each of her chipped fingernails, the collar of her blouse crumpled and unironed, a tiny cut on her cheek, a fringe that looked to have been cut with blunt nail clippers. I found a tissue and used it to wipe my sweating palms.

'How do you mean, just the square?'

'We sleep out in the square,' she said. She spread her hands to suggest the lie of her bed.

'Outside?'

She nodded.

'Tonight?'

'Yes.'

The memory of the bitter cold still tingled at my fingertips as I said, 'Why?'

It took her no more than two breaths to tell me the story. She and her brother had had to leave their country, Uzbekistan, when their parents – who were journalists – were arrested. It was arranged very quickly – friends of their parents acquired passports for them and put them on to a plane. They had been in England for three days but they knew no one here. This country was just a safe place. Now all the money they had could be lifted in the palm of a hand to a stranger in a toilet. So they were sleeping rough – in the shelter of a square, covered in blankets, on top of some cardboard.

At the next table a woman was complaining loudly that there was too much froth on her coffee. Her companion was relating the miserable tale of her daughter's attempt to get into publishing. What did they think about the strange girl sitting opposite me? Nothing. Only I knew what a menacing place Laylor's world had become.

She'd lost a tooth. I noticed the ugly gap when she smiled at me saying, 'I love London.'

She had sought me out – sifted me from the crowd. This young woman was desperate for help. She'd even cunningly made me obliged to her.

'I have picture of Tower Bridge at home on wall although I have not seen yet.'

But why me? I had my son to think of. Why pick on a single mother with a nine-year old? We haven't got the time. Those two women at the next table, with their matching handbags and shoes, they did nothing but lunch. Why hadn't she approached them instead?

'From little girl, I always want to see it...' she went on.

I didn't know anything about people in her situation. Didn't they have to go somewhere? Croydon, was it? Couldn't she have gone to the police? Or some charity? My life was hard enough without this stranger tramping through it. She smelt of mildewed washing. Imagine her dragging that awful stink into my kitchen. Cupping her filthy hands round my bone china. Smearing my white linen. Her big face with its pantomime eyebrows leering over my son. Slumping on to my sofa and kicking off her muddy boots as she yanked me down into her particular hell. How would I ever get rid of her?

'You know where is Tower Bridge?'

Perhaps there was something tender-hearted in my face.

When my grandma first came to England from the Caribbean she lived through days as lonely and cold as an open grave. The story she told her grandchildren was about the stranger who woke her while she was sleeping in a doorway and offered her a warm bed for the night. It was this act of benevolence that kept my grandmother alive. She was convinced of it. Her Good Samaritan.

'Is something wrong?' the girl asked.

Now my grandmother talks with passion about scrounging refugees; those asylum seekers who can't even speak the language, storming the country and making it difficult for her and everyone else.

'Last week...' she began, her voice quivering, 'I was in home.'

This was embarrassing. I couldn't turn the other way, the girl was staring straight at me.

'This day, Friday,' she went on, 'I cooked fish for my mother and brother.'

The whites of her eyes were becoming soft and pink; she was going to cry.

'This day Friday I am here in London,' she said. 'And I worry I will not see my mother again.'

Only a savage would turn away when it was merely kindness that was needed.

I resolved to help her. I had warm bedrooms, one of them empty. I would make her dinner. Fried chicken or maybe poached fish in wine. I would run her a bath filled with bubbles. Wrap her in thick towels heated on a rail. I would hunt out some warm clothes and after I had put my son to bed I would make her cocoa. We would sit and talk. I would let her tell me all that she had been through. Wipe her tears and assure her that she was now safe. I would phone a colleague from school and ask him for advice. Then in the morning I would take Laylor to wherever she needed to go. And before we said goodbye I would press my phone number into her hand.

All Laylor's grandchildren would know my name.

Her nose was running with snot. She pulled down the sleeve of her jacket to drag it across her face and said, 'I must find my brother.'

I didn't have any more tissues. 'I'll get you something to wipe your nose,' I said. I got up from the table.

She watched me, frowning; the tiny hairs of her

eyebrows locking together like Velcro.

I walked to the counter where serviettes were lying in a neat pile. I picked up four. Then standing straight I walked on. Not back to Laylor but up the stairs to the exit.

I pushed through the revolving doors and threw myself into the cold.

Introduction to
The Empty Pram

This story was commissioned by a woman's magazine. They wanted me to write a piece of about 1,000 words in length and make it easily accessible for someone who was not used to reading a lot. I took on the challenge.

I had just finished writing SMALL ISLAND and I still had a lot of stories in my head from my mum's experiences of first coming to England. Here was a chance to use one that I remembered well.

After completing the story I sent it to the person who had commissioned it. She was very pleased. We began the process of copy-editing that is necessary before anything is published. However, just as it was about to be approved, the editor of the magazine read it for the first time. She declared that this story was not suitable for her readers. Her readers, evidently, did not want to hear stories like this. It was too controversial.

The story was never published.

So be warned, this tale is too risky for the women of England!

The Empty Pram

HAVING JUST ARRIVED FROM Jamaica I was not ready for the strangeness of the encounter. It was 1948. I had been in England only three days and was eager to start my new life in this Mother Country. I was cleaning the scruffy room that my fool husband had rented for us to live in. What a run-down place it was; drab as a drink of water, and we had to share the bath with everyone else who lived in the house. There was a knock on the door. Just a gentle tap — so timid that at first I thought one of the rats had come to pay his respects. When I opened the door a little boy was standing there. Looking up at me with his mouth agape, he stood no taller than to my knees. And this boy was carrying a baby. Two skinny white arms awkwardly clasped it to his chest.

'What are you doing?' I asked him.

He grinned, showing me the gummy gap at the front of his mouth, 'This is my baby,' he said.

I had seen the boy before. He had been sitting at the front door when I had returned that morning from the shops. This English boy had white hair that sat straight up on his head as if he were upside down, and glasses so dirty that only one beady eye spied on me.

'Whose baby is that?' I asked him.

This poor baby was whimpering, for it was slipping down from the boy's grasp and was now being hugged tight round the neck. The boy was choking the baby.

'Did you carry it up all those stairs?' I asked.

The rascal boy nodded.

Now, the house in which I lived was a tall house. Six long flights of stairs to reach my room; I know, I had counted every step. My heart jumped with fretting at what could have befallen this baby climbing those stairs caught only in this boy's tender clutches. I went to lift the child from him but he did not want to give it up. While I placed my hands on the baby's chubby body, the boy tightened his grip around its neck. And we struggled there, the three of us, until finally I wrested the poor baby from him.

'Where is the baby's mother? Show me where you got the child from,' I said.

This boy, wailing now like I had just given him a good whack, ran down the stairs. I had no chance to catch him. So there was I left cradling this unknown baby.

I descended the stairs, tapping at each room door in the hope of finding someone who could help me in this plight. But there was no one in the house but me. The front door was gaping wide where the rude boy had run through. I followed him out into the street. There I saw a pram. Mothers in this country often left their babies outside so they might breathe some fresh air; they seemed to have no fear of it being abducted. Yet there was I holding a stolen baby. I went to the pram hoping to find it empty and my problem solved. But there, wrapped tight in blankets, was a peaceful sleeping infant. England was becoming a puzzle to me. Was no mother missing her child? I stood confused while the baby in my arms gurgled and dribbled.

Then I heard a scream. It was coming from around the corner. Following the sound of the commotion I saw a group of three English women looking aghast into another pram. An empty pram, I was sure. I rushed towards them.

'Is this your baby?' I said, as I approached the little group. Every one of those women looked on me with an expression so full of terror I thought to scream myself. Six eyes popped wide in their sockets and three mouths fell open at the sight of my black face. One of the women leaned to grab the baby from my arms. Then, clinging together, all three shielding the baby between them, they stepped smartly back away from me.

So I explained the situation. I told them about the boy bringing the child to my room. Expecting these women to release the held breath they had not dared to exhale, I smiled on them.

Instead their faces slowly creased into frowns as one of them said, 'I can't understand what's she saying.'

I repeated the tale, turning my attention to each of them as I spoke. But no comprehension lighted in their eyes. I said it again – louder this time.

One of the women puffed out her chest and began to put a roll on her sleeve. She stepped forward and grabbed my wrist – squeezing it tight.

'Get a policeman,' she said. 'She tried to steal the baby.'

I struggled with her, begging her to listen. But every

word I uttered caused them to fret more. I could not make myself understood.

'Police!' they shouted.

Then from around the corner came the little boy.

'There is the boy who had your baby,' I told this group.

This boy, seeing me standing there, proceeded to plead with these women. 'That woolly-haired woman took my baby,' he said. Then seeing the baby now in someone else's arms cried, 'That's my baby. I found it.'

'Where did you find it?' one of the women asked him.

'In the pram.'

'Did you take the baby out of this pram?'

The boy, finally realising he may have done something wrong, bit his lip and stared up into the air.

Oh, now they understood! 'Did he bring the baby to you?' I was asked.

I nodded.

'Oh, I see,' they said together.

The boy was given a quick slap around his ear. 'I've told you about that before, Georgie,' one of them said. 'Leave the babies alone.'

Another of the women started clapping her hands with relief that I was not the devil.

My wrist was released and the mother of the baby, who was smiling now, said, 'Thank you for bringing her back. But you should have told us what happened.' Then all three women began patting me like a dog – on the shoulder, on the head – as they discussed together whether I would like a nice cup of tea.

Afterword

Waterstones Bookshop asked me to write a short piece to accompany the month of February in a diary they were producing. My mum was my inspiration again. She has all the best stories.

February

WHEN MY MUM FIRST came to England from Jamaica she embarked on an evening class. She can't recall what the class was about but she can remember the essay she was asked to produce so her writing ability could be assessed.

'Describe winter in your own words', was the task my mum was set.

Now, not being very long in England, my mum was not that familiar with British winters. So she described the winters in Jamaica – her childhood Februaries. And there the 'Christmas breeze' blew its cooling air on her skin. Succulent avocado pears and soft ripe mangoes were at last upon the dining table. The ortaniques, stolen from the tree, squelched their sweet and sticky juice on to her fingers. In the garden the gentle early evening rains scattered droplets, bright as diamonds, on to the flaming red poinsettias. And the fragrant white euphorbia bloomed...

When my mum got this essay back from being marked she'd only got a C minus for all her effort. She was a little surprised. But then she read the reason written large in green ink.

'But this,' the teacher wrote, 'is not what February is like at all!'

Introduction to
Uriah's War

A relative recently told me that my grandfather had been at the Somme in France during the First World War. But I didn't believe it. I had never heard of Jamaicans taking part in that war. So I did some research. And indeed my grandfather was in the British West Indies Regiment during that conflict. I couldn't find any details of his service but he was probably on a labour battalion that supplied the front lines. Perhaps not in a combat position but in one that needed just as much heroism, as fatalities were high.

The centenary of the outbreak of World War One made me want to add the experience of West Indian troops to the record. The more I researched, the more I was struck by the patriotism and courage of the West

Indian men who volunteered to fight for the British Empire. This story is inspired by the experiences of soldiers of the 1st Battalion of the BWIR who fought in Palestine and Egypt. Their contribution must not be overlooked.

And I would like to acknowledge Richard Smith for his wonderful book *Jamaican Volunteers in the First World War*. Without it I would still not believe that my grandfather was at the Somme.

Uriah's War

AND WE FINALLY GOT to England. To the army camp at Seaford. Seaford? You know it? On the south coast? We had to sleep in the town, the place was under such mud. It rains grey all day – never go there. Well, there was this English man – white, you know – in a pub sort of thing; hotel taproom I think they call it. Me and Walker were sitting sipping on beer, when this man came to our table and stood above us to ask us a question.

'Why are you going to fight in this war for only a shilling a day?'

Now that sort of took the wind from me. And Walker's eyes – well, they shone with uneasiness; it would be us thrown from the place if there was trouble.

So we said nothing but this man still went on.

Churchill, Asquith and Lloyd George get pay of fifteen thousand pounds a year and we were fools to fight for the Empire because the King is German and all his family too.

Everyone staring on us, but we just sip, sip. And all the while I am thinking, a shilling is a lot of money. It took many a long time in Jamaica to earn a shilling. But I did not tell this man because he was looking to make mischief.

When two constables came in Walker braced himself, sure they'd come to seize us. But no. They marched out this Englishman, holding him rough stuff on either side. And he is now yelling on Walker and me:

'Lay down your arms... do not fight... white men should fight their own battles and black men theirs!'

They charged him: 'Making remarks likely to jeopardise recruiting to His Majesty's forces,' or some such. Sent him to prison. It is a true story. I might smile now when I recall but at the time Walker and me found nothing funny in it. Nothing funny at all.

He was belittling our patriotism.

And we were full of it then. Walker more than me. He was one of the first to volunteer for the British West Indies Regiment. He heard the King's appeal as if whispered by His Majesty into his ear alone: I ask you, men of all classes, to come forward voluntarily and take your share in the fight...

Walker was pleased that at last they would let black men do more for the King and Empire than ride a blasted bicycle around our island looking for spies.

You see, the Empire was our protector, that is how we thought. England was great, sort of thing. And she was under threat. You should have heard the stories of the barbarous Germans that swept the breeze. They were burning houses and churches and women and children. Some were eating babies. Well, that was one of the tales. Looking back now perhaps that was a little... embellished. But everyone believed it at the time.

It was Walker who persuaded me to join the colours with him. You see Walker is a big man. Over six feet. Taller than me, taller than most. He loves cricket. Seeing him bearing down upon you about to bowl a ball at your head, makes you want to sort of... well, run away. Cricket is his chance to show what he is made of. Every game he plays he plays to win. And that is how he prevail upon me. Our chance to show the British what black men can do. That was his creed. 'Buckle your armour for fight! Sons of the Empire rise'... sort of thing.

All my childhood memories have Walker standing in them somewhere. His mamma vowed that she was not his mamma but his auntie. One fool-fool tale did she weave of how Walker's parents perished in some misfortune involving a horse and cart. But all knew (and that included Walker) that he was the outside child of a big-big lawyer in Mandeville. A man renowned. An 'honourable' when he died, you know. But he did not recognise Walker as his son. So she concoct this elaborate tale so Walker would not be deemed of 'dubious birth'. If Walker minded her deception he did not say – he just calls her auntie because he wants to get on in this world. That is how he is. We worked together as clerks for a manufacturer's agent. Until he heard the call and we joined up! Two proud volunteers for the 1st Battalion.

Now, we thought all that parading around in freezing rain day after day at that camp in Seaford was our training for the battlefields of France. But when the order came to move we left England for Alexandria in Egypt.

Man, how Walker raged! Two days he bewailed me: what had he kept himself fit for? Was he not fitter than the puny-pale English boys we trained with (all fed on bread and dripping – whatever that is, we never asked them)? And had he not even so much as sneezed at that camp? (I got mumps – many of the boys from home did. Days I could not walk, I had such a swelling in… well, no matter.) His fight, Walker wanted everyone to know, his fight was with the Germans!

But our colonel made it quite clear that we West Indian troops would be labourers in France. Now, who wanted to come all that way to be in a labour battalion? Running back and forth with shells and what-and-what for the front line. No rifle, no combat, but just as likely to die. That would have been a humiliation.

It was great good fortune that our battalion joined the Egyptian Expeditionary Force. By the time we disembarked our ship for the camp at Mex, the Turk was our new firm foe. They were burning churches and houses and women and children. And Walker declared that the only worry we would have from him was to hold him back!

It was one hundred and twelve degrees in the shade as we marched across the Sinai Desert.

'Think of Moses', Walker say to me. 'Remember your Bible story? Moses pass over the Sinai. And he did not give up.' What was he chattin'? Moses could strike a rock and out would come water. One gallon was all our ration. My spittle was powder.

'Leave the stubble upon your face, so you have more water to drink. But sip it, sip it!' Oh how Walker nagged me through every march.

Even boys whose chests bulged from years of cutting cane found gouging out trenches in that terrain devilish work. And I was clerk! But so was Walker. Yet, he moved that desert aside like he was burrowing in his mamma's garden. As we laid cables for the front line we were bombed from the air. One boy on our section was burst by shrapnel. How he screamed! Walker had our machine gun rat-a-tat-tatting over that vast sky. While I soiled my pants. Not all black men are made from the same stuff, you know. Sometimes I wished on my friend, break, tremble, complain!

I staggered like a jackass, heaving the belts of bullets for the heavy Vickers gun that Walker just strode with balancéd upon his shoulder. Three days! Three days was all they gave us to learn that machine gun's tricks before we were put on operations at Umbrella Hill. Now, that was combat.

We were to raid the enemy's defences – fire trenches

and dugouts that were built up on the sand dunes behind barbed-wire entanglements three or four yards deep and just as high. The artillery's big guns made gaps in the wire while we formed a box barrage around the area. Walker and me were on the right flank. We hauled up our gun and ammunition to be ready for the order. You know what is an order? It is something that is easy to say and very hard to do. Reduce enemy manpower and capture and destroy enemy material.

Fifty rounds a minute we discharged. Shells were shrieking past us in their effort to destroy. Man, our gun heated so hot! Steaming smoke had Walker firing blind. I fed ammo into that gun while Walker shuddered to a blur with the force of firing. Every bullet on target. We were part of the machine! Invincible!

Then Gallimore's head blasted open. The force hurled our comrade into Walker. We had to wrestle him off, kick him out of the way. He rolled and bounced and I said, 'Sorry, man, sorry,' with every blow. Then I crawled over his bloody-dead body to get more ammo. And tried not to dwell upon the look I will find in his mamma's eyes when I get home.

One hundred and one men were counted dead that day. But that raid had those Turks on the run!

Walker slapped me upon the back. 'We break them, Uriah man, we break them!' And the light from his eyes nearly blinded me.

But the Turks are ferocious fighters. Fifty rounds a minute were not enough. They were waiting for us on the next raid.

We charged their trenches yelling like the famous Light Brigade. I lost Walker to my left and jumped into the Turks' works without him. A bomb exploded.

In the clearing dust I saw him up close. Dark as me! A Turk! Determined as me to kill. But I was quicker. My bayonet twisted in him before he raised his rifle. He fell at my feet. One more jab I gave him and seized the bomb he clutched from his hand. Then, and I don't know why, I punched him in the mouth.

Oh, how I wished Walker was there to see me. Proud is what he would have been. But instead five more Turks were advancing upon me, bayonets ready. I left that trench so quick! All around my comrades were retreating before this swarm of howling Turks.

They had us on the run now.

Shells exploded at the tip of my boot with every step I took. Those bombs pounded the land, rupturing it into mighty craters. I was trapped, locked between the savage Turk and this shrapnel barrage. No way back, no way forward. I stumbled into what should have been my grave.

Walker pulled me to my feet. Follow, he signalled. Follow! Man, he was fearless. He led round the flanks like he knew this ravaged land of old. Exhausted, bloodied and grateful, many of us made it back behind our lines.

Walker's coolness and devotion to duty was 'mentioned in dispatches'. And one of our officers, who had thought that black men would be no real help in this war, declared that we had jolly well changed his mind. Splendidly, he said we behaved, splendidly!

We fought those Turks so fierce that a big-big major remarked of us, 'My God! Are they angels or are they fools? Don't they see shells? Don't they hear shells, don't they know what shells are?' So amazed was he to see us West Indians passing through hails of exploding shrapnel like we were strolling to church. Our cheerfulness and our gallantry under heavy fire were heartily praised. And at the armistice we patted the backs of our imperial comrades – from Britain, New Zealand, Australia, India, Africa – and they patted ours.

'From over the seven seas the Empire's sons came...'

Our spirits could not have been higher when we got

to the camp at Toranto, in Italy. We are here to await our ship home. That is all. Walker and me had just arrived when a Jamaican private – with drooping eyes and a scowling mouth that told us he had been waiting for too long to leave this place – sidled up to us.

Black men are barred from using the cinema and the canteen at this camp, he told us. They are only for British Tommies with white skin. We black men are not allowed to sit amongst them. There had been trouble at this camp before and there would be trouble again, he said, because had we heard that all British Tommies had got a pay rise – from one shilling, to one shilling and sixpence a day? Walker and me rubbed our hands – that is a lot of money! But this man went on, no native unit was to receive this pay rise.

Now, Walker and me, as you know, are not from a native unit like this private. We had seen front-line service in Palestine. He had probably spent the war running back and forth with shells and what-and-what in a labour battalion. I did not tell the man this because he was looking to make mischief. But he then informed us that all West Indian battalions are classed as native units. Even those who had distinguished themselves upon the battlefields.

Now this sort of took the wind from me. But Walker raged.

Days he bewailed me. 'Did we not march up mountains? Freezing in our summer uniform with no water to drink?' he said.

'Yes,' I told him, 'but we are warm and well fed at this camp.'

'Did we not sleep nights without shelter? Bitter air benumbing us senseless. Waking each other every hour to check for warm breath and reason?'

'But Walker, we are only here waiting in readiness for our ship.'

'Did we not wrestle trucks through mud, sunk to our waists?'

'When we disembark in Jamaica we will find a hero's welcome.'

'How many of us died not from combat but malaria?'

'But come, Walker, we showed them what black men can do.'

'Have we not been bombed, shelled and shot at for the glory of the Empire?'

I begged Walker to calm himself.

But he is, at this moment, bound to the wheel of a gun carriage. Spread-eagled across it. His face pale. His eyes blackened. His lips bloated and sore.

We had been given an order by a sergeant, a white sergeant. And you know what is an order. We West Indians must clean out the latrines used by the Italian labourers of this camp.

What was this man chattin'? We all looked to each other. We must be hearing wrong. The white man has lost his mind. But no. Our order was to get pails and shovels and clean up the labourers' stinking shit.

And Walker's eyes... Oh, Walker's eyes!

He stepped out from us to stand before this sergeant. Walker is big man. And I feared for my friend. But he was polite. He was calm. He told the sergeant what we had been promised by our officers: we West Indians who had seen front-line service in Palestine would be spared all demeaning work. And work did not come more demeaning!

But this sergeant declared his orders were from the camp commander himself. The Brigadier General. And the general had said no such undertaking should have been promised to us West Indians. He could order us to do whatever work he pleased. And then this sergeant, this sergeant, he shout on Walker that we were better fed and treated than any nigger had a right to expect.

Well, Walker picked up a pail and threw it at this man's head.

Four white men then seized Walker. Threw him to the ground. Knelt on him. On his back. On his legs. His face was rubbing in the dirt. And he was struggling to fight them fierce. While the sergeant yelled on us black men that niggers should expect no more than this!

For disobeying an order, for attacking an NCO, Walker is on a Field Punishment Number One. My friend who was once mentioned in dispatches for his coolness and devotion to duty is shackled in fetters like a... like a slave.

I owe Walker my very life. But I am not permitted to approach him. Not even with water. So I intend to go to the sergeant to demand to speak to the Brigadier General about this injustice. Walker must be released. The most gallant and courageous soldier is being crucified under this charge.

Epilogue

I AM WALKER. And I write to inform you that my good friend Uriah Williamson has been shot dead. Killed by a sergeant attached to our own battalion. Uriah had approached this NCO to remonstrate against the punishment I had been put under. I believe, for I was tied up at the time, that Uriah spoke to the sergeant to make his case for my release. He was told that no such action would be taken and I would remain tethered. Uriah began to walk away but something changed his mind. He rounded upon the sergeant at such speed that this white man apparently feared for his life. He pulled out his revolver with the intention of warning Uriah to advance no farther. However, the weapon discharged. Uriah was hit in his heart. He died instantly.

There was tension at the camp in Toranto. There had been a mutiny before. The causes cited for that insurrection were again the demeaning tasks West Indian soldiers alone were ordered to perform. (A cause that led in no small part to my own FP no.1 punishment). The memory of this conflict stretched tempers and nerves on all sides. And one consequence was the death of my dearest friend.

Uriah was persuaded to join this war by me. But do not think him a coward deserving of scorn. His reluctance came from the fear that his beloved grandmother (with whom he lived) would have no one to reach the high shelves for her. But my persistence soon persuaded him. If we joined this battle then the King and Empire would be honour bound to reward our duty with equal treatment. Our sacrifice would see the black race uplifted.

His grandmother waved us off with a proud gaze. For Uriah and me had promised to one day bring all shelves to within her reach.

But I must state that I am alive to the fact that we West Indians were unfairly discriminated against in this war. This discrimination was not only an insult to all those comrades who volunteered to leave family and home, to fight, shed blood and die in foreign fields. But also an insult to the patriotism of the loyal people of the West Indies. Uriah and me did not fail you. We were British soldiers. But you have failed to recognise our contribution.

In consequence I turn my back upon Britain, my Motherland. The place I once believed was the seat of all that was good in my life. And turn my face to my island home of Jamaica. This war was fought for the principles of democracy and freedom. I now demand those principles for the black man. And to that fight shall all my energies be placed. For the right to vote, the right to work. But most of all, the right to live without insult.